HENRY PURCELL

Come, ye sons of art

(1694)

Birthday Ode for Queen Mary
Ode zum Geburtstag von Queen Mary

for SATB chorus, soloists and orchestra

Edited by / *Herausgegeben von*
ROBERT KING

FABER *ff* MUSIC

ISBN 0 571 51556 8

This edition © 1995 by Faber Music Ltd
First published in 1995 by Faber Music Ltd
3 Queen Square London WC1N 3AU
Cover design by S & M Tucker
Music processed by Donald Sheppard
Printed in England by Halstan & Co Ltd
All rights reserved

Orchestra

2 Trumpets/2 Trompeten
2 Treble Recorders/2 Alt-Blockflöten
2 Oboes/2 Oboen
Violin 1/Violine 1
Violin 2/Violine 2
Viola/Viola
Basso continuo

Duration c. 26 minutes
Spieldauer ca. 26 Minuten

Full score available on sale (0 571 51557 6) or hire
Parts available on hire

Come, ye sons of art is recorded by Gillian Fisher, James Bowman,
Michael Chance, Michael George, the Choir of New College, Oxford,
and The King's Consort, directed by Robert King
on Hyperion CDA 66598

Introduction

From between 1680 and 1695 twenty-four of Purcell's Odes and Welcome Songs survive: four celebrate St Cecilia's day, six are for the welcome of royalty, three are for the birthday of King James II, six celebrate the birthdays of Queen Mary from 1689 to 1694, and the remainder are 'one-offs' for a royal wedding, the Yorkshire Feast, the birthday of the Duke of Gloucester, the Centenary of Trinity College Dublin, and one for a performance 'at Mr Maidwell's School'. Full of wonderfully inventive music, many have been quite unjustly ignored. Besides their musical value, the works have an added interest for the scholar as they cover almost the whole period of Purcell's activity as an established composer; his first Ode, for the welcome of Charles II, dates from 1680, and his last (that for the six-year-old Duke of Gloucester) was written just a few months before the composer's untimely death in 1695.

Purcell composed six Odes in successive years from 1689 to celebrate the birthday (on April 30th) of Queen Mary. Like the majority of the British public, Purcell was genuinely fond of Mary, who, with her husband William of Orange had replaced King James II on the throne when he fled to the Continent. *Come, ye sons of art* (1694) was the composer's sixth and final offering to the Queen, who succumbed to smallpox at the end of the year. This ode is markedly different from the majority of the preceding twenty-two works. The forces utilised were larger than usual, with an orchestra replacing the more usual single strings, and a more clearly defined role for the chorus. Purcell's recent successes on the stage may have encouraged this more expansive style of composition: the inspired text (probably by Nahum Tate), full of references to music and musical instruments, fired Purcell's fertile imagination.

Performance

Come, ye sons of art is splendidly adaptable in performance. It works well (and was probably first performed) with choir, soloists and orchestra, but is equally successful with much smaller forces: a double quartet of eight good singers (between them taking all the solos), together with single strings, two recorders, two oboes and two trumpets (or one) can produce a thrilling result. The orchestral string disposition will vary according to the size of the choral forces, but a period instrument string section of 4 first violins, 4 second violins, 3 violas and 4 bass violins is ideal. For modern instrument orchestras two or three cellos could be substituted for the bass violins (a larger form of cello, often tuned a tone lower and producing a darker, richer sound). In solo sections just one cello should play. The double bass was almost certainly not used in Purcell's performances (though one or two of the bass violins would, at special moments, drop down an octave): the timbre of this 8'-based orchestral scoring is wonderfully transparent and well worth trying. The mansuscript instructs that the Symphony at bar 178 be played by 'flutes': in Purcell's day this terminology always meant recorders. The bassoon was just appearing in English orchestras around this time, but its presence here does not seem necessary.

For chordal continuo instruments Purcell would have probably had at his disposal harpsichord, chamber organ and theorbo: for more gentle movements the intimate sound of organ and theorbo is ideal. A written-out keyboard continuo part (see Full Score) has been supplied by the editor: it has also been figured for the benefit of more experienced players. When no orchestra is available, the keyboard reduction (prepared by Silas Standage) offers an effective alternative for performance with organ. Organists should, at their own discretion, redistribute or expand the given reduction to make use of the pedals.

Trills should always start on the upper note, and should be prefaced by a long appoggiatura: that appoggiatura is more important than the actual trill, which should always be seen as an elegant, French grace note, and never as a device which intrudes on the melodic line. For full Introduction and source details, please refer to the Full Score.

Robert King

Einleitung

Von Purcell sind aus den Jahren zwischen 1680 und 1695 24 Oden und *Welcome Songs* überliefert: vier dieser Werke feiern den Tag der Heiligen Cäcilia, sechs weitere haben den Empfang königlicher Gäste zum Anlaß, drei sind für den Geburtstag von König Jakob II. geschrieben, sechs zelebrieren die Geburtstage von Königin Maria (Queen Mary) in den Jahren von 1689 bis 1694 und die übrigen, die jeweils für sich alleine stehen, entstanden zu diversen Anlässen, nämlich für eine königliche Hochzeit, das Yorkshire Fest, den Geburtstag des Herzogs von Gloucester, die Hundertjahrfeier des Trinity Colleges in Dublin und für eine Aufführung 'an Mr Maidwell's Schule'. Viele dieser Werke, die voller hervorragender musikalischer Einfälle stecken, sind zu Unrecht vernachlässigt worden. Die Werke haben neben ihrem musikalischen Wert für den Wissenschaftler noch einen zusätzlichen Reiz, umspannen sie doch fast vollständig Purcells Wirkungszeit als anerkannter Komponist: seine erste Ode, zum Willkommen für Karl II. komponiert, ist 1680 datiert, seine letzte Ode (für den sechsjährigen Herzog von Gloucester) wurde erst einige Monate vor dem unerwartet frühen Tod des Komponisten 1695 geschrieben.

Purcell komponierte in jährlicher Folge ab dem Jahr 1689 sechs Oden zu Ehren des Geburtstages von Königin Maria (am 30. April). Wie die Mehrheit der Engländer, verehrte auch Purcell die Königin Maria, die mit ihrem Ehemann, Wilhelm II. von Oranien, König Jakob II. auf dem Thron abgelöst hatte, als dieser auf den Kontinent floh. *Come ye sons of art* (1694) war die sechste und letzte dieser kompositorischen Gaben an die Königin, die Ende 1694 den Blattern erlag. Die Ode unterscheidet sich deutlich von der Mehrheit der vorangehenden 22 anderen Oden. Purcell verlangt eine größere Besetzung – die üblicherweise einfach besetzten Streicher sind hier zu einem Orchester erweitert – und weist dem Chor eine klarer umrissene Aufgabe zu. Dieser üppigere Kompositionsstil mag durch Purcells erst kurz zurückliegenden Erfolg als Komponist von Bühnenwerken veranlaßt gewesen sein: der wahrscheinlich von Nahum Tate geschriebene, geistreiche Text, der voller Anspielungen auf Musik und Musikinstrumente steckt, regte Purcells musikalische Phantasie stark an.

Aufführungspraxis

Come, ye sons of art läßt sich in der Praxis auf vielfältige Weise realisieren. Das Stück klingt in einer Besetzung mit Chor, Solisten und Orchester gut – so wurde es wohl auch zuerst aufgeführt. Es ist aber auch in kleinerer Besetzung wirkungsvoll; mit einem Doppelquartett von acht guten Sängern, die untereinander die Soli aufteilen, begleitet von einfach besetzten Streichern, zwei Blockflöten, zwei Oboen und zwei Trompeten (oder nur einer), läßt sich ein faszinierendes klangliches Ergebnis erreichen. Wenn das Werk durch ein Orchester begleitet wird, wird die Streicherbesetzung je nach der Größe des Chores schwanken, ideal ist aber die Interpretation durch historische Instrumente und zwar mit vier ersten Geigen, vier zweiten Geigen, drei Bratschen und vier Baß-Violinen. Bei einem aus modernen Streichinstrumenten bestehenden Orchester könnten zwei oder drei Celli die Baß-Violinen ersetzen (eine größere Art Cello, oft einen Ganzton tiefer gestimmt und mit einem dunkleren, wärmeren Klang). Bei Solo-Abschnitten sollte nur ein Cello begleiten. Der Kontrabaß fand sicherlich in Purcells Aufführungen keine Verwendung (obwohl es üblich war, eine oder zwei Baß-Violinen bei besonderen musikalischen Abschnitten um eine Oktave nach unten zu versetzen). Das Timbre dieses im Achtfußregister gehaltenen Orchestersatzes ist von besonderer Durchsichtigkeit und lohnt einen Versuch.

Das Manuskript schreibt für die *Symphony* in Takt 178 *'flutes'* vor: Zu Purcells Zeit bedeutet ein solcher Hinweis immer Blockflöten. Das Fagott tauchte zur Zeit Purcells in englischen Orchestern gerade auf, sein Einsatz hier wird als nicht notwendig angesehen.

Als akkordisches Continuo-Instrument dürfte Purcell ein Cembalo, eine kleine Orgel und eine Theorbe zur Verfügung gehabt haben; für die zarteren Sätze ist der intime Klang von Orgel und Theorbe besonders geeignet. Eine Continuo-Aussetzung wurde vom Herausgeber ergänzt. Diese Aussetzung wurde zusätzlich auch beziffert, um den fortgeschritteneren Spielern die Möglichkeit zu geben, nach Akkordziffern zu spielen. Sollte ein Orchester nicht zur Verfügung stehen, ermöglicht der von Silas Standage angefertigte Klavierauszug eine praktikable Alternative für die Aufführung mit Orgelbegleitung. Der jeweilige Organist sollte den mitgeteilten Klavierauszug nach eigenem Gutdünken anders aufteilen oder entsprechend ergänzen, um sein Pedal einzusetzen.

Triller sollten immer auf der oberen Nebennote beginnen und durch einen langen Vorschlag eingeleitet werden; dieser Vorschlag ist wichtiger als der eigentliche Triller, den man immer als eine elegante Verzierung in französischer Manier und nie so ausführen sollte, daß er die eigentliche Melodielinie undeutlich werden läßt. Die vollständige Einleitung und Hinweise zur Quellenlage finden sich in der Partitur.

Robert King
Deutsche Übersetzung: Dorothee Göbel

Come, ye sons of art

Birthday Ode for Queen Mary, 1694
Ode zum Geburtstag von Queen Mary, 1694

[Nahum Tate]

Henry Purcell
1659 – 1695

sons—of art, come, come a-way, Tune all—your voi-ces, and— in - stru-ments
sons—of art, come, come a-way, Tune all—your voi-ces, and in - stru-ments
sons of art, come, come a-way, Tune all—your voi-ces, and in - stru-ments
sons of art, come, come a-way, Tune all your voi-ces, and in - stru-ments

play, To ce-le-brate, to ce-le-brate this tri-um-phant day. Tune all— your
play, To ce-le-brate, to ce-le-brate this tri-um-phant day. Tune all— your
play, To ce-le-brate, to ce-le-brate this tri-um-phant day. Tune all—— your
play, To ce-le-brate, to ce-le-brate this tri-um-phant day. Tune all your

voi - ces, and in - stru - ments play, To ce - le - brate, to ce - le - brate this

voi - ces, and in - stru - ments play, To ce - le - brate, to ce - le - brate this

voi - ces, and in - stru - ments play, To ce - le - brate, to ce - le - brate this

voi - ces, and in - stru - ments play, To ce - le - brate, to ce - le - brate this

poco rall.

tri - um-phant day, to ce - le -brate, to ce - le -brate this tri - um-phant day.

tri - um-phant day, to ce - le -brate, to ce - le -brate this tri - um-phant day.

tri - um-phant day, to ce - le -brate, to ce - le -brate this tri - um-phant day.

tri - um-phant day, to ce - le -brate, to ce - le -brate this tri - um-phant day.

poco rall.

155

You make the list'n - ing shores re - sound,_____ re - sound,

___ you make the list'n - ing shores re - sound,_____

157

the list'n-ing shores re - sound.

___ you make the list'n - ing shores re-sound.

160

2.

-sound. On the spright - - ly haut-boy, the

-sound. On the spright - - ly haut-boy, the spright-ly haut - boy play, the

12

Repeat SYMPHONY (bb. 60–87) and CHORUS (bb. 116–143)
(Source reads "Sym. & Chorus again")

Man wiederhole SYMPHONY (Takte 60–87) und CHORUS (Takte 116–143)
(Hinweis in der Quelle: "Sym. & Chorus again")

pa - tron - ess - es praise, sing your pa - tron - ess - es

praise, sing, sing, sing, sing. In cheer — — — — — — —

RITORNELLO

— — — ful and har-mo — nious lays. lays.

FULL

just-ly seems to crave, Grant, oh grant, grant, oh grant, and let it

have, let it, let it have, let it have the ho - nour of a Ju - - bi - lee.

zeal best__ in-structs you how to pray,__ how__ to pray,__ how_____ to pray, Hour-ly from her own, her own con-vers-ing, con-vers-ing, con-vers-ing with the e - ter - - - - - - - - nal, the__ e - ter - nal__ throne.

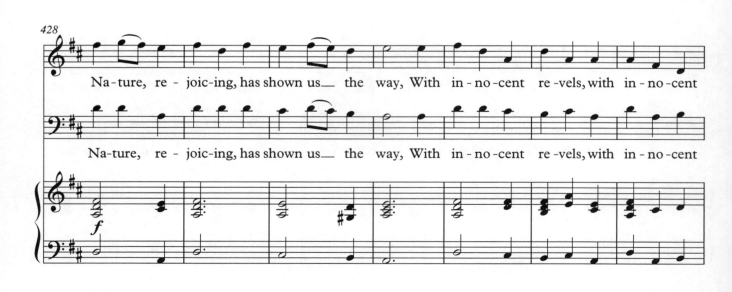

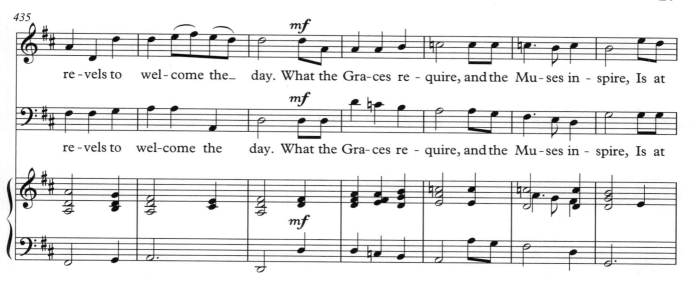

re-vels to wel-come the_ day. What the Gra-ces re - quire, and the Mu-ses in - spire, Is at

re-vels to wel-come the day. What the Gra-ces re - quire, and the Mu-ses in - spire, Is at

once our de - light and our du - ty_ to_ pay. Thus Na-ture, re - joic-ing, has

once our de - light and our du - ty to pay. Thus Na-ture, re - joic-ing, has

shown us_ the way, With in-no-cent re-vels, with in-no-cent re-vels to wel-come the_

shown us_ the way, With in-no-cent re-vels, with in-no-cent re-vels to wel-come the

shown us— the way, With in -no-cent re -vels, with in -no-cent re -vels to wel-come the—

shown us the way, With in -no-cent re -vels, with in -no-cent re -vels to wel-come the

shown us the way, With in -no-cent re -vels, with in -no-cent re -vels to— wel-come the

shown us— the way, With in -no-cent re -vels, with in -no-cent re -vels to wel-come the

day. The tune - ful— grove, the talk - ing rill, the laugh - ing vale, re -

day. The tune - - ful grove, the talk - ing rill, the laugh - ing vale, re -

day. The tune - ful— grove, the talk - ing rill, the laugh-ing, the laugh - ing—

day. The tune - ful— grove, the talk - ing rill, the laugh - ing vale, re -

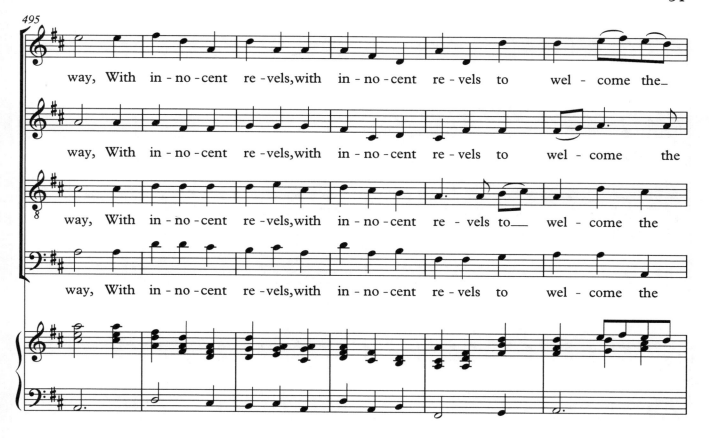